THE VOICE OF MY MIND

ARSHYA PRINJA

With gratitude

to

Divya Prinja and Ashish Prinja

(Mom and Dad)

Thank you for showing me my hidden talent and motivating me
to start this journey!

Contents

1. Choco Snack

*(Being a big chocoholic I had tried this chocolate for the first
time and loved it so much that I wrote a poem on it.)*

*The one who made that chocolate should get an accolade.
The yum-yum cream that makes me scream!
Chocho is its name and should come on the list of fame.*

Its cute packing, makes me start flapping.
Every child likes chocolate,
without knowing that it was every Mayans biggest fate!
The one who made that chocolate should get an accolade.
The yum-yum cream that makes me scream!
But the dentists on the other hand saw their fate,
when they could see the cavities higher rate!
The one who made that chocolate should get an accolade.
The yum-yum cream that makes me scream!

Written on the 26th of December 2020

---

2. The Sky is Blue

In nature, nothing is perfect and everything is perfect. Trees can be contorted, bent in weird ways, and they're still beautiful.
—Alice Walker

The sky is blue and the flowers are white,
everybody say that nature is always right.
From winds that blow everytime,
to us humans making words rhyme.
We never take care of our nature,

without thinking that it's our future.
The sky is blue and the flowers are white,
everybody say that nature is always right.
From the Sun which is very bright,
to the flowers living without any fright.
We are worse than all creatures,
even if we have teachers.
The sky is blue and the flowers are white,
everybody say that nature is always right.

Written on the 31st of December 2020

---

3. Going to the Roads

Going to the Roads,
where everybody rarely goes.
The tall-tall trees,
and the cold breeze.
Seeing the rising Sun,
and eating a yummy bun.
Going to the Roads,
where everybody rarely goes.

Small little shops,
and looking at the flying flocks.
Reading a book,
and saying bye to the customer the bus just took!
Going to the Roads,
where everybody rarely goes.

Written on the 14th of September 2020

---

4. Should I bathe Today?

Winter day Bath

The most relatable ongoing saga in winters - 'Being scared of taking a bath.'

On a very foggy day,
you ask yourself should I bathe today?
Those hours of rubbing,
those seconds of shivering.
Those hours of rapid reflex actions,
which turns your natural heat into fractions.
On a very foggy day,
you ask yourself should I just take a sponge today?
Those hours of relaxing,
and those seconds of dancing.
Maybe I should just have a sponge today!

Written on the 24th of Septemer 2021

---

5. Sheriff

Sheriff is my dog. This photo was when he was just 42 days old.

A dog is a man's best friend they say,
maybe I took the right way.
Looking at Sheriff my furry friend,

makes my sadness to reach it's end.
His wet nose and fur that's gold.
Looking at Sheriff my furry friend,
makes my sadness to reach it's end.
After a long dark day,
looking at Sheriff makes the Sun's rays come my way.

Written on the 5th of April 2021

---

6. Bubbles

*Let's take inspiration from those airy bubbles that lift up in the
sky,
sometimes they also pop but still do not cry.
They soar up in the sky with the help of the wind,
but go in the opposite direction maybe they have their own
wings.
They tell us not to uprise to high or will get popped by the air,
overconfidence is the bad habit we all humans share.*

Wind is like their overconfidence that makes them pop,
but keep working on your goals don't make it your full stop!
Let's take inspiration from those airy bubbles that lift up in the
sky,
sometimes they also pop but still do not cry.

Written on the 29th of April 2021

---

7. Home Syndrome

Corona is making us sit at home,
making us all have home syndrome.
With all these troubles we are having today,
maybe there is something nature wants to say.
Maybe she wants us to realize by,
giving us back our own crimes.
Corona is making us sit at home,
making us all have home syndrome.
People now say life is pale,
let's not give up before we say that we failed.

Life can be happy,
life can be sad,
it's nature's way it can't be that bad.
Corona is making us sit at home,
making us all have home syndrome.
This break is something we can't fill,
with sadness or with a will.
We will get out of this soon,
fighting together will be our boon!
Corona is making us sit at home,
making us all have home syndrome.

Written on the 14th of May 2021

---

8. Man of Fun

Man of fun and likes to run,
wears specs and looks perfect!
It is my mamu double the fun,
his face shines like the sun.
Sometimes shabby hair and beard,
but I can't remember a person he hasn't cheered.
Fan of eggs, hairy legs.
Man of fun and likes to run,
wears specs and looks perfect!
Can make any frown upside down,
is the exact copy of a clown.
Can make history as fun as PE,
it's something he can do freely.
He is just like John Cleese,
can cook anything as yummy as cheese.
Man of fun and likes to run,
wears specs and looks perfect!

Written on the 16th of May 2021

---

9. Parents Day!

Why say I love you only on Mother and Father's day?
I love you is something I should say to you every single day.
Mom, you are there for me,
even if you are not free.
Dad, you are the technosavy guy,
but also eat the ice cream which is actually mine!
I can't imagine one day in your place,
cause what you do can bring tiredness to your face.
Why say I love you only on Mother and Father's day?
I love you is something I should say to you every single day.

Written on the 23rd of July 2021

---

10. Peace

"Do not let the behavior of others destroy your inner peace."
—Dalai Lama.

The fear in the eyes,
the abandoned child that cries,
a mother looking for shelter,
people running helter-skelter.
The sight gives me a shiver,
would you like to be there ever?
I dream of a world where all,
will know the freedoms way,

where there is no greed in the soul,
nor revenge fills our day.
Come it's time to decide,
in which world do we want to reside?
We can right the wrongs,
we can sing more songs,
for much joy in this world,
PEACE is the word.

Written on the 1ˢᵗ of February 2022

---

11. Rejuvenation

"Our physical, emotional, and spiritual health requires rest. We need to take a break. We need to nurture ourselves. To take a time out to refuel, rejuvenate, and revive ourselves."

Life is filled with ups and downs, happiness, and tears,
But we slowly learn how to fight our fears.
We learn from our mistakes,
From the wrong turns we make,
From the fake friends we make,
And from times we almost break
It's time to accept your flaws,

Otherwise fear will catch you in its paws
I have seen my parents in tension,
But they never mention
I think it's time for them to rejuvenate,
Playing some music would be great!
Remember your childhood,
When you used to be happy with the food.
Do things again, like you are doing it for the first time,
Enjoy it once again and then no thought would begrime.
Dance and jump again like you are a teen,
and sing in the shower like you are insane.
Beauty, money, and luxuries won't accompany you to the grave,
But a contended heart and soul and the memories you made.
Rejuvenate your thoughts like the rising sun,
And life would be more fun.

Written on the 5th of May 2022

---

12. Anshuman

Anshuman ,my brother.

Annoying and slightly cute,

works as a part-time brute.
Always talking about dinosaurs and cars,
can identify any car from afar.
Space is his new love,
but he is always the brat I will love.
Seeks help from me in Minecraft,
but I just talk as if I am daft.
He's my 24/7 friend,
and my love for him will never end.

Written on the 5th of June 2022